Winner of the Maxim Mazumdar New Play Competition

A PATCH OF EARTH

a courtroom drama of the Bosnian war

by Kitty Felde

Chesapeake Press

For Tad, my best critic and biggest fan.

And thanks to all the lawyers, judges, translators, legal scholars, and most of all, witnesses who stepped forward to create the international community's first foray into justice for the victims of war crimes since the Second World War.

CAST OF CHARACTERS

Drazen Erdemovic - 24

Vesna Erdemovic - his young wife - (also Operator at American Embassy)

Father Erdemovic - (also plays Brano the calm commanding officer, and Jovan Babic, the Serbian defense attorney)

Mama Erdemovic - (also plays the Judge)

Elsbeth Van der Kellen – the Dutch prison guard (also plays Voice 2)

Julija - Drazen's old girlfriend - (also plays Newscaster 2)

Stanko - Erdemovic' nemesis (also plays Newscaster 1, and Guard 2)

Aleksandar - dumb kid who joined the army - (also plays Bailiff, voice 3, Philip)

Prosecutor - (also plays Soldier, bus driver, Voice 4, French Reporter, and Old Man)

All available actors play ghosts. All the women play the whispered voice of Nevin.

PRODUCTION NOTES

The play is performed without accents.

There is no definable set for this play, since most of the events take place in the mind and memory of Drazen Erdemovic. Shifts in setting are created with lights and sound.

The cast plays multiple roles. Characters from different periods of Erdemovic' life drift in and out on stage – much like his thoughts and worries. The stage is also inhabited from time to time by the ghosts of Srebrenica's dead, played by various members of the cast wearing similar grayish burlap garments.

The voice of the child Nevin is performed by the female cast members as a chorus.

There is no intermission.

PRONOUNCIATIONS

Aleksandar - Alexander
Bejelina - bay-ya-LEEN-uh
Babic - BAH-bich
Brano - BRAH-noh
ciscenje (cleansing) - cheesh-CHEN-ye
Croat - CROW-at
Cvetkovic - SVEHT-koh-vich
dinars (currency) - DEE-nahrs
Dobro jutro (good morning) - DOH-broh YOO-troh
Drazen - DRAW-szhen
Erdemovic - air-DEM-oh-vich
glupak (imbecile) - GLOO-pack
Gojkovic - GOY-kah-vich
gospodine (Sir) - ghos-poh-DEE-nay
jongen - (boy) - YAWNG-uhn
Julija - YUHL-ya
Juffrouw - (Miss) - yuh-FROW
kurac (penis) - KOO-rats
Maastrict - MOSS-strict
Maja - MY-yah
Mauritskade - MOW-ritz-skahd
Medjugorje - MEHD-juh-GHOR-jia
nazdraviti (to your health) - nahs-draw-VEE-tee
obstina (county) - ahb-SHTEEN-uh
oprostite (sorry) - oh-PROHST-eet-eh
Pilica - PEE-lee-tza
pivo (beer) - PEE-voh
rakia (brandy) - RAH-kee-ya
Savanovic - sih-VAHN-uh-vich
Scheveningen – SHAY-vehn-ing-ehn
slivo (plum brandy) - SLEEVE-oh

Srebrenica - SHREH-breh-NEET-za
Svetkovic - SVEHT-koh-vich
Tito - TEE-toe
Ustashe - oo-STAH-shuh
Vesna - VEHS-nuh
Willem - VILL-uhm
Zanic – ZAH-nich

The play begins in the dark. We hear echoes of voices.

VOICE 1: Erdemovic!
VOICE 2: Erdemovic!
VOICE 3: Erdemovic!
VOICE 4: Erdemovic!

ERDEMOVIC: I am Drazen Erdemovic!

GUARD 1 taps his wooden baton on the metal bars. The lights come up on what appears to be a jail cell. We see 24 year old DRAZEN ERDEMOVIC. He's a short kid with acne scars and a hip haircut.

Erdemovic jerks awakes from his nightmare, covered in sweat.

GUARD 1: Hey! Hey! Keep it down in there! You'll wake up everybody else in detention. (to another guard)The kid sounds terrified.
GUARD 2: Wouldn't you be?

We hear three slow taps of a gavel on wood. The lights become much brighter. The stage has become the courtroom.

BAILIFF: The International Criminal Tribunal for the Former Yugoslavia is now in session. Please be seated.

The two guards escort Erdemovic to an area down center. They stand on either side of him. A handsome 50-something man in a long black robe joins them.

This is Jovan Babic, the defense attorney. He nods to Erdemovic.
Up center, on a platform behind a scrim, a red-robed female judge appears. On either side of her are silhouetted outlines of two fellow judges.

JUDGE: The Tribunal must now ask you whether you plead guilty or not guilty.
ERDEMOVIC: Your honor, I have told my counsel that I plead guilty to crimes against humanity.
BABIC: Your honor, my client is a victim of the whirlwind of war – and the victim of his own deed.
JUDGE: Mr. Erdemovic, you have heard the version of the facts which the prosecutor has just stated. Do you agree with what he said?
ERDEMOVIC: I agree with everything that the prosecutor has said. And I have more to add.
JUDGE: Mr. Erdemovic. You will be given the opportunity to speak at a later time.
ERDEMOVIC: Your honor, I had to do this. I had no choice.
JUDGE: Mr. Erdemovic!
ERDEMOVIC: If I had refused, I would have been killed together with the victims. My comrades told me, "If you're sorry for them, line up with them and we'll kill you, too." I'm not sorry for myself, but for my family – my wife and son.

The lights come up on Vesna and Nevin, Erdemovic' young wife and child, in their 'house' in another part of the stage. Vesna stands over a wooden cradle, slowly tearing a piece of paper into small bits. Vesna sings to the "child" in the cradle.

VESNA (sings): Papa's gone to be a soldier
Gone to fight the evil ogre
Tiny baby sleeps
In silent castle keeps
Lying on a downy bed of clover…

The lights fade on Vesna.

ERDEMOVIC: My son. He was only nine months old. (he openly weeps) I couldn't refuse because then they would have killed me. That is all I wish to add.

The judge is clearly uncomfortable.

JUDGE: All right, Mr. Erdemovic! Try to get hold of yourself! Sit down for a moment. Please sit down for a moment.
BABIC (whispers): Drazen! Drazen, please! The worst is now over. You must be quiet!
ERDEMOVIC: No. I can be silent no longer.

We hear the three gavel pounds. The lights fade. They come up again at the Father's front door. Erdemovic enters, carrying a heavy television set. It's obviously not brand new. He juggles the set and pounds on the door.

ERDEMOVIC: Mama? Mama, are you home?
MAMA: Drazen? Drazen, is that you?
ERDEMOVIC: Open up, Mama. I'm a Croat bearing gifts.

Mama opens the door wide. She laughs with delight when she sees the TV set.

ERDEMOVIC: Happy birthday, Mama.
MAMA: Drazen!

She kisses him on both cheeks, over the television set.

MAMA: Just wait until I show this to Sylvana! She who brags so often about *her* fancy television set.
ERDEMOVIC: It's not so fancy, Mama.
MAMA: It's fancy enough for me. Any more buttons, I would never learn how to make it work.
ERDEMOVIC: Happy birthday, Mama.

She kisses him again.

ERDEMOVIC: Let me in, Mama. Let me put this down before I drop it.
MAMA: Come in, come in!

Erdemovic struggles to get the set through the door. As he puts it down on a table, he looks up to see his father standing there, watching, not offering to help, his arms crossed over his chest.

MAMA: See who's here to celebrate my birthday!
ERDEMOVIC: Father.
FATHER: Drazen. Shopping again, I see.
ERDEMOVIC: For Mama's birthday.
FATHER: From one of your 'clients', I suppose.
ERDEMOVIC: They couldn't take it with them when they crossed the border. I offered them a fair price.
FATHER: I'm sure you did.
ERDEMOVIC: Better than leaving it behind for someone to steal.
FATHER: Yes indeed. Better to steal it yourself.
ERDEMOVIC: I told you, I paid them –
FATHER: Yes, I heard. You paid them a fair price.
ERDEMOVIC: Something you always did, Father, I'm certain.

MAMA: You should be proud, Papa. Your son taking after you, an entrepreneur through and through.
FATHER: Drazen always finds a way to make a dinar. Even in the middle of a civil war. What exactly do you call this line of business you are in these days?
ERDEMOVIC: I'm in transportation, Father. I told you.
FATHER: Transportation. Smuggling cowards across the border is more like it. And what happens when you get caught?
ERDEMOVIC: I won't get caught.
FATHER: For your mother's sake, I hope not. But knowing you, Drazen, I wouldn't put any money on it.
ERDEMOVIC: What's that supposed to mean?
FATHER: You haven't exactly had a sterling track record when it comes to your many careers.
ERDEMOVIC: There is a war going on, Father.
MAMA: And Drazen did serve in the army, Papa. Remember?
FATHER: I remember he came home with his tail between his legs, boo-hooing about the harsh treatment he received.
ERDEMOVIC: I had to leave.
FATHER: Yes, I know. Army food wasn't as good as the fine meals your mother makes.
ERDEMOVIC: There were maggots in the gruel. The meat was rancid.
MAMA: Who wants a bite of my plum cake? Drazen?
ERDEMOVIC: No, thank you, Mama.
MAMA: Papa?
FATHER: No, thank you.

There is an uneasy silence. Erdemovic plugs in the television set and fiddles with the antenna. There is a lot of static.

FATHER: Look, Drazen. You are a bright boy.
ERDEMOVIC: (he scoffs) Puh.
FATHER: Come here, boy. I know I'm hard on you. Too hard, perhaps. But you're my best and my brightest. I just wish you

would use those brains. It makes me angry when you take the easy way out.
ERDEMOVIC: Easy way? You think sneaking families over the border is easy?
FATHER: It's another of your "get rich quick" schemes. With no thought for the future.
ERDEMOVIC: What future? It's easy for you to talk, Father. You lived your life under Marshall Tito. Your future was secure. What kind of future is out there for me? My country is splitting apart and the only place that wants my talents is the army.
MAMA: Well, I for one, am glad Drazen is no longer in the army. I would not sleep at night, worrying about my boy.
FATHER: He's not a boy, Mama. He's a married man. (under his breath) He's certainly no soldier.
ERDEMOVIC: No, I'm not, Father. Why should I be? Why should I kill anybody? Just to prove to you that I am a man? This war is craziness. I have no stake in it. Why should I fight?
FATHER: You are afraid.
MAMA: Papa –
FATHER: A coward.
MAMA: Enough!
FATHER: A crybaby.
ERDEMOVIC: Goodbye, Mama. Happy birthday.
MAMA: Drazen!

He starts to leave.

FATHER: If they catch you, Mr. Crybaby, they'll send you to the front. And then what will your mother think?

Erdemovic slams the door.
We hear the three taps of the Tribunal courtroom gavel. The lights change.

JUDGE (voice) Mr. Erdemovic, you pleaded very much the cause of peace. At the same time, you happened to join all the fighting groups during this war. Wasn't there any other way to express your belief in co-existence?
ERDEMOVIC: Your honor, we were forced to join the army. Who was I? Just simple Drazen Erdemovic. No one would listen to me. Nobody asked me whether I wanted to join the army. Only those with enough money could buy out their lives. People with cafes, with petrol stations, those with small businesses. They could buy their way our of the army. Not me. Not Drazen Erdemovic. I didn't want the war. I had no motivations to go to war. If I did not join willingly, they would have taken me anyway and sent me to the front lines. That's the situation in the Republika Srbska. You follow orders or there are fateful consequences. (pause) Is there anyone here who can understand me? My wife is a Serb. It's not her fault she's Serb and I'm Croat. It's not her fault Serbs are waging war. Was I supposed to hate her because she's a Serb? Is there anybody here who can understand me?

The lights go to black. A moment later, they fade up to very dim light. We see Erdemovic splashing water from a bowl onto his face. He dries his face on a towel and reaches for a uniform shirt. He starts to put it on. He hears a threatening voice.

VESNA: Stop right there, Drazen Erdemovic.

He freezes.

VESNA: Thought you could get away with it, did you?

VESNA enters. She is a young woman in a nightgown. She approaches Erdemovic from behind, putting her arms around his chest, under his shirt.

VESNA: Running away in the dark without even saying goodbye.
ERDEMOVIC: I didn't want to wake you.
VESNA: Well, I'm awake now. What are you going to do about it?

He finishes putting on the shirt, her arms still entwined around his body. He turns around and kisses her.

VESNA: Come back to bed.
ERDEMOVIC: I can't. I'm late.
VESNA: Who cares? Let them wait. Tell them – tell them you have official duties - much more important duties to perform. Come back to bed.
ERDEMOVIC: I don't think my commander would understand official duties performed without a uniform.
VESNA: Then leave your uniform on. Or most of it, anyway.

She starts undressing him.

ERDEMOVIC: Vesna, stop. I really have to go.
VESNA: Then go! You would rather spend time with your comrades instead of your dull wife and child.
ERDEMOVIC: Not so.

He kisses her gently.

VESNA: Stupid army.
ERDEMOVIC: Stupid army that found us a home to live in.
VESNA: Home! Barely a house. They could have been more careful with their mortar shells, making holes in the roof where the rain pours through.
ERDEMOVIC: It's better than nothing. It's better than having our baby out under the plum trees.

VESNA: It's not fair. To have to live like this. Like peasants. I dream of a real home, Drazen. A house where there are electric lights and a toilet that flushes. Look at us, Drazen! We're living the life of our great-grandparents!
ERDEMOVIC: Things will get better.
VESNA: That's what you always say! Things never get better.
ERDEMOVIC: It was not so long ago that we had nice things.
VESNA: Yes. And now all the nice things are gone – gone to buy food and diapers and toilet paper. All that money they paid you, Drazen – deutschmarks and dinars and dollars. You were a such an important man! Like your father.
ERDEMOVIC (bitterly): Like my father. The businessman.
VESNA: You were the real businessman, Drazen. A tour guide, really, taking clients across the border on a Swiss holiday. For that they throw money at you with both hands. Both hands!
ERDEMOVIC: We were greedy, Vesna. We got caught.
VESNA: Is it greedy to want something better for our little boy? I remember you in the disco, Drazen. Flashing dinars around like they were paper money. Everyone paid attention to you. Everyone. The eyes of every girl in the disco were on Drazen Erdemovic, the boy with the dinars. And now, look at us. Look at you! Working as a stupid soldier for a stupid army that is not even your own.
ERDEMOVIC: Would you rather have me in prison? The penalty for smuggling is 20 years behind bars.
VESNA: You don't know that for sure. The world is upside down. You don't know they would carry out the sentence.
ERDEMOVIC: Oh, I know.
VESNA: All I know is that <u>you</u> chose to enlist. We should be in Switzerland, not them. All those neighbors you helped across the border. People you risked your life to save! If they had been true friends, they wouldn't have turned their backs on us, pretending we didn't exist.
ERDEMOVIC: They weren't our friends, Vesna. They were people with a few thousand deutschmarks to spend on safe passage to somewhere away from the fighting.

VESNA: Yes, and now they're all safe in Switzerland. And where are we? Stuck in the middle of a war that will never end. And now you are marching off to die.
ERDEMOVIC: I'm not going to die, Vesna. I'm too smart for that.
VESNA: (she laughs) You're not that smart, Drazen. Nobody's that smart.

He kisses her, trying to reassure her. She pouts for a moment, but then kisses him back. Her anger is gone, replaced by fear and longing. They hold each other for a few moments. And then there is the distant sound of rocket fire. We see the reflected glow.

VESNA: Listen. They light up the sky with their rockets.
ERDEMOVIC: It's time for me to go.

Erdemovic pulls away.

VESNA: Damn the Muslims. And damn the Serbs. And damn the Croats, too. Who am I supposed to hate, Drazen? Who is your son supposed to hate? You are Croat. I am Serb. Who is your son supposed to hate?
ERDEMOVIC: I have to go.
VESNA: What is it this time?
ERDEMOVIC: Srebrenica.

The lights fade to black.

Lights up on a television reporter and a cameraman. The video of this is broadcast on a large screen television that appears behind the scrim stage left.

NEWSCASTER 1: Dutch peacekeeping troops today pulled out of the U.N. safe area of Srebrenica. About 400 soldiers abandoned their mission of trying to protect 25 thousand Muslim men, women and children from the army of invading Bosnian Serb troops. Thousands of Muslim men were loaded onto busses and driven away from the U.N. safe area. The Dutch U.N. commander says he's received assurances from the Bosnian Serb military commander that the men will not be harmed.

The cameraman changes angle to shoot another reporter.

NEWSCASTER 2: Another mass grave was discovered late yesterday in a remote forest outside the town of Srebrenica. Forensic investigators say the ditch carved out of an abandoned soccer field may hold as many as 200 bodies…

Papa Erdemovic enters the stage. Both reporters and the cameraman surround him. Again, the action is "broadcast" on the large screen television.

PHILIP: Mr. Erdemovic. Sir? I wonder if I could talk to you about your son. Your son, Drazen Erdemovic?
FATHER: Reporters! Leeches! Go away! Leave me alone! I lost the best I had. He should die. Let him die. At least I would know where he was buried. I don't need him alive. He's better off dead.
REPORTERS: Mr. Erdemovic! Mr. Erdemovic! Mr. Erdemovic!

The reporters chase him offstage as the lights fade out. There is the sound of a truck motor. The lights come up on the back bed of a rag-tag military truck, seemingly bumping along a country road. This is a low platform at center. It later becomes the jail cell and the bed for Drazen & Vesna.

The troops are jolly, singing a dirty Serbian song and slapping each other on the back. Erdemovic runs alongside and is helped up by one of his comrades. Erdemovic sits next to STANKO, legs hanging off the end of the truck. BRANO stands quietly, holding onto the cab of the truck. He doesn't sing.

BRANO: Glad you could join us, Sergeant Erdemovic.
ERDEMOVIC: Sorry, sir.
BRANO: I notice you didn't bother to shave this morning.
ERDEMOVIC: Sorry, sir.
BRANO: I should make you run behind the truck for a few kilometers.
ERDEMOVIC: Sorry, sir.

The men tease him by chanting "sorry, sorry" in sing-song Serbo-Croat.

MEN: Oprostite. Oprostite. Oprostite.
BRANO: Enough!

He bangs on the cab window.

BRANO: Turn left here.

The crowd in the truck leans to the right as the truck 'turns'.

STANKO: Where are we going, Commander?
BRANO: A little target practice.
ALEKSANDAR: Another drill? I've been in this army three months and all I ever shoot are stacks of hay and scarecrows.
BRANO: Be careful what you wish for, Private.
ERDEMOVIC: (quietly) Stanko.
STANKO: Something wrong, comrade?

ERDEMOVIC: You ever kill anybody?
STANKO: (he winks) A few jealous husbands.
ALEKSANDAR: Hah! When are you gonna share your secrets of your kurac, Stanko?
STANKO: When you're old enough to know what to do with one, glupak. (he slaps Aleksandar on the side of his head. To Erdemovic:) How's that wife of yours, comrade?
ERDEMOVIC" Fine. Fine.
STANKO: Prettiest girl in the disco. Prettiest girl in the obstina.
ERDEMOVIC: I don't know if I can do it, Stanko.
STANKO: Do what?
ERDEMOVIC: Shoot someone. Kill someone.
STANKO: Just remember they're the bad guys. We're the good guys.
ERDEMOVIC: I've never seen anyone die before.

The 'truck' has stopped. The soldiers start to jump off, leaving Erdemovic and Brano behind. Brano slaps Erdemovic on the back.

BRANO: Buck up, Erdemovic. Today's your lucky day.

Brano jumps off and exits. The light remains on Erdemovic for a moment, the lights go to black.
Lights up on the Prosecutor.

PROSECUTOR: Your honor. Drazen Erdemovic, present here in the courtroom today, was a soldier in the tenth sabotage detachment of what was then the Bosnian Serb army. This unit was ordered to a farm near the village of Pilica. There, he was ordered to receive busloads of Muslim civilian men who had surrendered, or had been apprehended fleeing from Srebrenica. They were brought by these busses to this remote farm on the day of 16th of July 1995. The soldiers ordered to this farm were given the task to summarily execute the civilian men.

PROSECUTOR: (cont) These executions resulted in the deaths of hundreds of Muslim men. Drazen Erdemovic was a member of this squad. He did what he was asked to do. These, your honors, are the facts behind the indictment.

The lights go out. We hear the sound of keys in a heavy metal lock. The lights come up on Erdemovic' jail cell. Erdemovic is lying down, with a "how to get rich" book over his face. A female guard enters. She is very tall, broad shouldered, and blonde.

GUARD: Lunch time.
ERDEMOVIC: I'm not hungry.
GUARD: Sure you are.
ERDEMOVIC: Go away.
GUARD: Sorry. No can do. It's my job to make sure all detainees eat a hearty lunch.
ERDEMOVIC: What are you? Designated detention mother?
GUARD: That's right.
ERDEMOVIC: Too bad. I'm still not hungry.
GUARD: Suit yourself. (pause) It's pea soup. Local delicacy.
ERDEMOVIC: Please leave me alone.
GUARD: Sorry.

Erdemovic goes back to his reading. The guard starts whistling.

ERDEMOVIC: Excuse me. Excuse me!
GUARD: What? Oh, sorry.
ERDEMOVIC: Do you harass all the detainees this way or just me? What's your name?
GUARD: Why? You gonna report me?
ERDEMOVIC: Maybe.
GUARD: Officer Elsbeth Van der Kellen. (she salutes) Sir!
ERDEMOVIC: Sir. I like that. Army, huh?

GUARD: Yup. Look. I'm not trying to bother you. I'm just trying to cheer you up.
ERDEMOVIC: And what do I have to be cheerful about?
GUARD: You're alive. You've got a good solid Dutch roof over your head. (she leans in to whisper) And they don't believe in the death penalty at the Tribunal.
ERDEMOVIC: I feel so much better.
GUARD: Good. So what else can I do to cheer you up? Another book? How about a game of ping pong? Maybe I can requisition a gameboy.
ERDEMOVIC: You really want to do something for me?
GUARD: I know. Go away and shut up.

He sits up with the thought.

ERDEMOVIC: A letter. You can write me a letter.
GUARD: A letter?
ERDEMOVIC: That's right.
GUARD: Okay. A letter to the newspaper? Or maybe to the prison warden?
ERDEMOVIC: A letter to my wife. Every day.
GUARD: All – all right. What do you want me to say?
ERDEMOVIC: Ask her to come visit me. Here in Holland. Here in prison.
GUARD: Don't you think she'd rather get a letter from you yourself?
ERDEMOVIC: She does get letters from me. Every day.

He reaches in his pocket and pulls out a torn letter.

ERDEMOVIC: And every day, they come back. Torn into little pieces.

He dumps the contents of the box and tiny pieces of letters tumble out like snow.

The lights fade on the actors, though we can still see the pieces of letters falling to the ground. The lights come up on the house portion of the stage where the bits of paper have become autumn leaves falling to earth. The cradle is onstage and we hear the child babble to himself. Erdemovic quietly enters the yard, stands for a few moments to watch his small son. Vesna walks outside to dump a pan of water.

ERDEMOVIC: Vesna?

She is surprised and drops the pan, which startles the child, who starts to cry.

VESNA: Drazen? Drazen, you're home! Drazen!
ERDEMOVIC: (he breaks into tears) Vesna. Vesna.
VESNA: Shh. Drazen. Hush. You'll make Nevin cry as well.

Nevin carries on.

VESNA: You see? Nevin, you silly boy. Don't you recognize your own papa?

The child cries even louder.

VESNA: Hush, Nevin. Shh. It hasn't been that long. You remember your papa. (to Drazen) He acts as if he's seen a ghost.
ERDEMOVIC: Maybe he has.
VESNA: You're talking nonsense. (she touches her hair) Oh, look at me. No! Don't look. Here, let me put Nevin to bed while you go tell your parents you are home. Go, quickly! I saved a nice piece of meat for dinner. Maybe I knew in my heart you were coming home today. You are home for good, Drazen?
ERDEMOVIC: Good or bad. I'm home.

Vesna takes the large rag doll that is Nevin inside the house. Erdemovic leaves his bag on the steps and walks over to his father's house, where we hear the sound of a staticky television program. His Father pounds on the side of the set.

FATHER: (calling offstage) You see, Mama? I am just as clever with my hands as I am with my brain. A little bang on the side was all it needed. Not that there's anything to watch these days. Maybe we'll be lucky and there will be a football match.

He clicks through the various channels. They are all news programs.

FATHER: (calling) Sorry, Mama. No luck today. There's nothing but propaganda from that lot in Belgrade.
ERDEMOVIC: Father?

Father looks up. He is caught off guard. He is genuinely relieved and happy to see his son come home in one piece. He starts to embrace him, remembers himself, and pulls back. He and Erdemovic awkwardly shake hands.

FATHER: Drazen. Drazen, my son, is it really you?
ERDEMOVIC: Hello, Father.

Embarrassed, Father calls for Mama.

FATHER: Mama. Mama! Look who's here!

Mama rushes in and embraces Erdemovic.

MAMA: Drazen! Thank the Lord. Let me look at you. No bullet holes. No scars. But what is this uniform?
ERDEMOVIC: Mama, I told you. Bosnian Serb.
MAMA: (she spits) That's what I think of your Bosnian Serb uniform. You are Croat. Not Serb. Why don't you serve in your own people's army?
FATHER: You remember, Mama. That was last month. This is our son who wears the uniform coat of many colors.
ERDEMOVIC: It's a job, Mama. That's all. I had no choice.
FATHER: Choice? You always have a choice, Drazen.
ERDEMOVIC: Do you, Father? Do you really?
MAMA: Don't start arguing again. Not today. This is a celebration. A homecoming. We must toast our son, home in one piece, thanks be to God.

She finds three slightly chipped glasses and puts them on a tray. Father takes his favorite chair. Erdemovic hovers nearby. He can't sit still. Suddenly, out of the darkness up center, one of his ghosts appears. It is a man in gray, with a burlap sack over his head. Erdemovic leaves the window and returns to where his father is reading the paper.

ERDEMOVIC: And how are you doing, Father?
FATHER: How am I doing? What am I doing is more like it. Nothing. Not a damned thing! Every factory in the country has stopped making anything useful. How can you export fine furniture when there is not a spring to be had for love or money? And who would want to buy a chair from a country that doesn't exist anymore? I tell you, this country went straight into the toilet the day Tito died.

Mama hands around the brandy.

MAMA: Enough politics, Papa. We drink to Drazen, home at last.
FATHER: To Drazen. To my son. Nazdraviti!

They drink. Another ghost appears. Erdemovic shakily puts down his glass and walks to the window.

ERDEMOVIC: Father. Do you remember grandfather's war?
FATHER: Your grandfather was not a Nazi sympathizer!
ERDEMOVIC: I never said he was. But Father. In the army, I heard stories I never heard at home. Stories about grandfather's war.
FATHER: Rumors. Just rumors.
ERDEMOVIC: Perhaps. But such stories, Father. Stories of ciscenje – ethnic cleansing they call it now. The Serbs remember a massacre on St. Vitus Day, near Medjugorje. Six hundred women and children thrown off the cliff near the Franciscan monastery. And the story of a Croatian law student who won a special competition by slitting the throats of more than 13 hundred Serbs, using a special knife. They say he received a gold watch and a roast suckling pig for his service to the Croatian people.
FATHER: Lies! All Chetnik lies! Your grandfather was Ustashe, it is true. But he was a true patriot. A fighter for the Croatian people, a true crusader for our people and our holy Catholic church.
ERDEMOVIC: I've never seen you in church a day in your life.
MAMA: Drazen. Drink your rakia and leave your father alone. He is tired.
FATHER: What do you want from me?
ERDEMOVIC: I want to know what grandfather said about the war. Did he ever follow orders he knew were wrong? Did he ever have to follow orders that made him sick?
FATHER: Your grandfather put the war behind him when he came home. Never talked about it again. That's good advice, Drazen. You are home now. What happened happened. Take off that uniform and go home and kiss your wife.

Erdemovic starts to say something else, but catches a message in his mother's eyes. He kisses her on the cheek and leaves the house.
He starts to walk home, but hears loud laughter and Serbian juke box music down the street. He enters the smoky bar – full of patrons – and is immediately kissed by JULIJA. Erdemovic is surprised. They both laugh.

ERDEMOVIC: Julija, you little witch! I didn't know you were working here.
JULIJA: Working here. I own the place! Drazen, it's so nice to have you home again!

She kisses him again.

ERDEMOVIC: Careful. I'm a married man these days.
JULIJA: Oh, yes. And where is the precious Vesna?
ERDEMOVIC: Home with the baby.
JULIJA: You used to be such a fun fellow, Drazen. The king of the disco, we used to call you. Marriage doesn't look good on you, Drazen. Especially marriage to precious Vesna.
ERDEMOVIC: Julija.
JULIJA: No, no. You can see I'm not a bitter woman. I have learned to lose at love with humor and grace. Though why I ever brought Vesna to come with me that night is a mystery to me. She was a stick in the mud even then. God, we were young!
ERDEMOVIC: Your hair was long then. Down to your hips. You shouldn't have cut it.
JULIJA: Too hard to keep clean during the siege. Too many buckets of water. Not enough soap.
ERDEMOVIC: It's still nice.

JULIJA: Thank you, gospodine Erdemovic. (she assumes a John Travolta-like stance, remembering their disco days) Do you remember that nickname?
ERDEMOVIC: (he laughs) It was a long time ago. Ancient history. I'm making a vow not to live in the past. Not to ever look back. Let's drink to the future, Julija. You have the honor of serving me my first beer now that I'm back home.
JULIJA: With pleasure. One pivo.

She starts to exit. Erdemovic grabs her hand and pulls her into a disco dance pose. They both laugh and she exits.

STANKO: Why don't you join me over here, comrade?
ERDEMOVIC: (a bit out of breath) Stanko!

Stanko slowly crosses the room. He is drunk.

STANKO: That's right, old friend Savanovic Stanko. Such a reunion of old army comrades requires a celebration, does it not?
ERDEMOVIC: Stay away from me, Stanko. I am no longer a soldier.
STANKO: Ah, contraire, my old friend. You are forever a member of the tenth sabotage detachment. And as your closest comrade, I'm going to buy you a drink. Julija! Two more pivos! And here I thought I'd lost track of you, old friend.
ERDEMOVIC: Leave me alone, Stanko.
STANKO: Have a seat, comrade.

They walk over to a table.

STANKO: (laughs) Somehow I knew I'd find you here. After you bragged to the rest of us soldiers of weaker character that you were going to give up drinking. Now that you're a married man.
ERDEMOVIC: I've had trouble sleeping lately. I thought a drink would help.

STANKO: What's wrong, old friend? The little wife isn't giving you enough exercise at home? (he laughs again)

Julija plunks down two beers.

JULIJA: You have cash this time, Stanko?
STANKO: Where's your faith in your fellow man, Julija?
JULIJA: I place my faith in anything that fills the empty spaces in my cash register.

Stanko laughs and slaps down several coins on the table. Julija scrapes them up and walks away.

STANKO: So. Did your family give you the homecoming of your dreams?
ERDEMOVIC: My mother spits on my uniform. My son stares at me as if I am a stranger. No. Not just a stranger. As if I'm a menace. A monster. He screams when I pick him up.
STANKO: You let him get away with that and you'll have problems later. Listen to Papa Stanko. You just have to let him know who's the boss of the family.
ERDEMOVIC: And you are such an expert? "Papa" Stanko?

A ghost enters and takes a seat at the bar.

STANKO: Who's to say how many children I have fathered in the line of duty?

Erdemovic stares at the ghost.

ERDEMOVIC: Stanko. I can't stop thinking about it.
STANKO: About what?
ERDEMOVIC: You know what. I keep seeing the blood under the cornstalks. I keep seeing their eyes. I hear them, Stanko. Every night in my dreams.

STANKO: Pull yourself together, comrade. You are a member of the tenth sabotage detachment of the Bosnian Serb army. Remember that.

The ghost exits.

ERDEMOVIC: What about you? Is it so easy for you to forget about it?
STANKO: Forget? Never. I want to remember every drop of blood I spilled that day. Every drop.
ERDEMOVIC: How can you live with that?
STANKO: Listen, comrade. Those stinking Turks killed my brother. Shot him before he even reached his 18th birthday. This was my chance to pay them back. I should have just buried them alive and not wasted the bullets.
ERDEMOVIC: Stanko, how do you know it was those men who killed your brother?
STANKO: How do you know they didn't? (pause) I got 253 of them at Pilica farm. Two hundred fifty three stinking Turks and it still isn't enough to equal the man my brother never grew up to be. I was the one who had to tell my mother that her favorite son was not coming home. I was the one who had to look her into her eyes. Like staring at a frozen river. Nothing but ice. But underneath, everything is black and rushing somewhere I can't see. Everywhere I go, I am haunted by those eyes.
ERDEMOVIC: But, Stanko. So many bodies. So many people killed. It wasn't a battle. It was a slaughter.
STANKO: It was smart soldiering. Killing them right there and then meant they couldn't come back and kill another day. Less bad news to deliver to sad Serbian mothers.
ERDEMOVIC: Who's delivering the news to sad Muslim mothers?
STANKO: That's the beauty of it. Nobody. Nobody's delivering the bad news. That's because there are no witnesses! No proof. Just another case of troops missing in action. For all those U.N. fellows know, our Turkish friends just left the country.

STANKO: (cont) Emigrated to parts unknown. Parts unknown. That's pretty good. (he laughs. And then he stops) You don't have plans to talk to those Muslim mothers or anyone else about our little mission?
ERDEMOVIC: Why would you say that?
STANKO: I have a bad feeling about you, comrade.
ERDEMOVIC: I can hold my tongue.
STANKO: You'd better, my friend. Because the fewer witnesses left alive to talk means the rest of us have to worry that much less. Understand?
ERDEMOVIC: I get it. I've got to get home to my family.
STANKO: All the more reason for you to keep your mouth shut. You wouldn't want anything to happen to that nice wife and kid of yours, would you?

Erdemovic rises.

ERDEMOVIC: You stay away from my family, Stanko. I'll kill you.
STANKO: Yes. You're pretty good at killing, aren't you? Not as good as me, though. You just don't have the stomach for it.

He calmly rises and walks over to Erdemovic. And punches him in the stomach. Erdemovic gasps.

JULIJA: Drazen!
STANKO: That's to put something solid in that soft stomach of yours. Adios, comrade.

Stanko leaves the bar.

JULIJA: Drazen, can you breathe?

Erdemovic is again weeping.

JULIJA: Drazen?
ERDEMOVIC: Leave me alone, Julija. Please. Just leave me alone.

She does. The lights fade on the bar. Lights come up on the central platform. It has become the bedroom of Erdemovic and Vesna. She enters with a quilt and lays down beside him. The cradle is in the downstage corner. A clock strikes three. Two ghosts also enter and sit across the room. Erdemovic is tossing in his sleep.

ERDEMOVIC: No. I won't do it. Do you hear me? I won't do it! No!
VESNA: Drazen. Wake up. Drazen, it's only a dream. Shh! Wake up.

Nevin screams in his sleep. Their dreams seem to intersect.

ERDEMOVIC: What? What!!?
VESNA: This house is full of nightmares.

Nevin continues to scream.

ERDEMOVIC: Nevin. I'll see to him.

He lights a lamp and stumbles over to Nevin's cradle.

ERDEMOVIC: Hush. Hush, Nevin. It's only a dream. Shh.

He brushes the child's hair out of his eyes. He sings to Nevin.

ERDEMOVIC: Papa's gone to be a soldier
Gone to fight the evil ogre
Tiny baby sleeps
In silent castle keeps
Lying on a downy bed of clover…

We hear the voice of Nevin. It is the whispered chorus of all three female actors.

NEVIN: Papa?
ERDEMOVIC: Yes, little one. It's your Papa.
NEVIN: Monster.
ERDEMOVIC: All gone. Papa killed the monster. All gone.
NEVIN: All gone?
ERDEMOVIC: That's right.
NEVIN: Papa monster.

Erdemovic nearly sobs.

ERDEMOVIC: No. Not a monster. Your Papa was a soldier, Nevin. Just a plain soldier.
NEVIN: Papa monster.
ERDEMOVIC: Nevin, stop it. I'm not a monster. I'm not. Please believe me.
NEVIN: Papa monster. Papa monster.
ERDEMOVIC: No. No! Shut up, shut up, shut up, shut up!

He shakes the child violently.

ERDEMOVIC: You know nothing! Nobody can know what it was like! They turned us all into monsters. All of us!

Erdemovic realizes what he is doing and freezes. He clasps the child to his chest.

ERDEMOVIC: My God, I am the evil ogre! Nevin. Nevin, my sweet plumkin.. Please forgive me.
You must forgive your poor Papa. Nevin? Can you ever forgive me?
NEVIN: (muffled) Papa monster.

Erdemovic realizes that they are not alone. Slowly, Erdemovic turns around and sees a pair of ghosts. He realizes that Nevin sees them, too.

ERDEMOVIC: My God! (he turns to the ghosts) Go away! Leave us alone!

But the ghosts stay where they are.

ERDEMOVIC: What do you want? My life? My soul?
NEVIN: Papa monster?
ERDEMOVIC: Papa's not a monster, Nevin. Not so. Don't believe them. Is it my fault I tried to save my life? Am I to be blamed for that? I did not want to shoot them. (he touches the boy's hair) That boy. That one young boy. His hair stuck out on all sides of his head, just the way yours does when you wake up from a nap. He was so scared. So scared he even peed in his pants. Just the way you do, Nevin. He was such a funny looking fellow. Barely a teenager. And yet, God help me, Nevin, I shot him dead. I shot him dead. I am so very, very sorry, Nevin. Please, please, forgive your papa.

He sobs.

NEVIN: Don't cry, Papa. Monster gone.

Erdemovic looks up and notices the ghosts have gone. He again clutches the child to his chest.

ERDEMOVIC: Monster all gone. All gone. Monster all gone.

Erdemovic staggers back to bed. His murmuring wake Vesna.

VESNA: Monster? What monster? Drazen.
ERDEMOVIC: Hmm?
VESNA: Drazen, what are these dreams you keep having? Every night.
ERDEMOVIC: Nightmares. Just nightmares.

The ghosts return. There are three of them this time.

VESNA: Maybe you should talk to someone. Maybe Father Zanic.
ERDEMOVIC: No one. I can talk to no one.
VESNA: You can talk to me. Drazen, please. Tell me what is wrong.

He sees the ghosts. They nod at him. He swallows.

ERDEMOVIC: Vesna, what stories did you hear about Srebrenica?
VESNA: A victory for our troops.
ERDEMOVIC: Yes. A victory. Do you know what that means?
VESNA: It means you came home, alive and in one piece.
ERDEMOVIC: Do you ever think about them?
VESNA: Them?

The ghosts are everywhere. Listening.

ERDEMOVIC: The ones we're fighting. The ones who won't come home in one piece because we shot them full of holes
VESNA: It is none of my concern. You and Nevin are my concern.

ERDEMOVIC: Vesna. What is the worst thing you can ever imagine?
VESNA: Drazen. Don't play these games.
ERDEMOVIC: The very worst.
VESNA: All right. You're not coming back from the fighting.
ERDEMOVIC: Worse than that.
VESNA: Losing our little Nevin. God protect us all.

She crosses herself, touching her forehead, then chest, then right and left shoulders. Erdemovic rises and walks away from Vesna and the child.

ERDEMOVIC: What would you say if you knew I had done worse. Much worse.
VESNA: Drazen, you're scaring me. Stop it.
ERDEMOVIC: Vesna. Look in my eyes. Have I changed since coming home?
VESNA: No. No, of course not. You're a little thinner. A little browner.
ERDEMOVIC: Look at my hands, Vesna. Can you see the blood on them?

The ghosts rise.

VESNA: Stop it.
ERDEMOVIC: I killed them, Vesna. I killed them all. Shot them in the back one by one by one. Bang. Bang. Bang. Bang. Bang. Bang. Bang. Bang. Bang.

One by one, the ghosts fall down. The lights fade out as we hear Erdemovic' litany of "bangs".
Overlapping his "bangs," in the dark, we hear the sound of a gavel pounding three times.

Lights up on the courtroom. The "judges" appear upstage. Erdemovic is escorted by his ghosts to the docket.

BAILIFF: The International Criminal Tribunal for the Former Yugoslavia is now in session. Please be seated.
PROSECUTOR: Mr. Erdemovic. Are you able to estimate how many people you killed on July 16th in that cornfield outside of Srebrenica?
ERDEMOVIC: I don't know exactly. But to be quite frank, I'd rather not know how many I killed. There was an elderly man. Between 50 and 60 years of age. When he came out of that bus, he said he had saved Serbs.

One of the ghosts steps forward. He takes off his mask. He is this older man.

OLD MAN: Please. Please! You must listen to me.
ERDEMOVIC: Why?
OLD MAN: I saved them. Lots of them.
ERDEMOVIC: How?
OLD MAN: Smuggled them across the border.
ERDEMOVIC: For cash, I suppose.
OLD MAN: I saved Serb lives! Dozens of them. Me, a Bosniak, saving Serbs. I took them to safety across the border. I never lost a soul. Doesn't that count for something?

Brano enters and walks over to Erdemovic and the Old Man.

ERDEMOVIC: Captain? Uh, this old man here says he's saved a lot of Serbs.
OLD MAN: Please, Captain. I can prove it. I have names and phone numbers. Please. Let me live!

Erdemovic turns to the judges to plead his case. The Old Man and Brano remain in their tableau.

ERDEMOVIC: I wanted to save that man. I was simply sorry for those people. I had no reason to shoot them. They had done nothing to me. But my commander. He didn't want to have any witnesses to that crime.
BRANO: Shoot him.
ERDEMOVIC: No, sir. Please. He is a good man. He saved Serbs. He has proof. Surely that is enough to let him live.
BRANO: Shoot him now.
ERDEMOVIC: But sir!
BRANO: The chief doesn't want to leave behind a single living witness.

Brano leaves the stage. Erdemovic and the Old Man are left to stare at each other. The Old Man slowly puts back on his sack mask. The lights change again.
Erdemovic returns to his cell. The Guard enters with an envelope.

GUARD: Mail call.
ERDEMOVIC: I don't even want to see it.
GUARD: Buck up, Erdemovic. We've already x-rayed the thing and it's definitely not a bomb. What's the worst it could be?
ERDEMOVIC: You open it.

She tears open the envelope. And looks inside. Sadly.

ERDEMOVIC: Don't tell me, let me guess. Torn into eight perfect little pieces. Vesna is nothing if she isn't neat.
GUARD: I'm sorry.
ERDEMOVIC: So am I.

GUARD: Maybe tomorrow –
ERDEMOVIC: I have no tomorrows.

The lights come up on the Erdemovic' bed. Vesna brings breakfast in bed.

VESNA: Wake up, sleepyhead.

Erdemovic groans and rolls over.

VESNA: Drazen. I know you can hear me. Come on. You can do it. Open your eyes. Look what I brought you. Breakfast in bed.

Erdemovic slowly wakes up.

ERDEMOVIC: I'm so tired.
VESNA: I'm not surprised. No one sleeps in this house anymore. It's one continuous nightmare.
ERDEMOVIC: I'm sorry.
VESNA: I just don't understand why you are the only one who believes there was a massacre at Srebrenica.

A ghost joins them. Erdemovic sees it. Vesna does not.

ERDEMOVIC: I was there, Vesna.
VESNA: Yes, but the news people say the stories are just Muslim propaganda.
ERDEMOVIC: Why would anyone make up a story like that?
VESNA: The world hates the Serbs. It always has. This is just more manufactured proof that Serbs are the villains.
ERDEMOVIC: Manufactured proof.
VESNA: How do you know those so-called missing men in Srebrenica aren't just hiding out, trying to avoid military service? How do you know they haven't just emigrated to Germany?
ERDEMOVIC: I saw the bodies, Vesna.

VESNA: In your dreams. In your nightmares, you saw those bodies. It's not real, Drazen. It's all in your head.
ERDEMOVIC: No.
VESNA: Where's the evidence, Drazen? How many people did you say your unit supposedly shot? 12 hundred? Where are the bodies? Surely you'd remember disposing of 12 hundred bodies.
ERDEMOVIC: I saw the bulldozers driving down the highway. Big yellow machines. To dig hundreds of bodies into the ground.
VESNA: And why has no one found these giant holes?

Erdemovic rises and moves away.

ERDEMOVIC: I don't know.
VESNA: Why are you the only one who talks of such things, Drazen? Surely if it had truly happened someone else would have told such a story.
ERDEMOVIC: People are scared.
VESNA: I'm scared, too.

She rises and goes to him.

VESNA: I'm scared you're slipping away from me. Slipping away from all that is real. Drazen. Look at me. Look around you. This is real. Your home. Your family. Your wife. Touch me, Drazen. I am real. (she holds him close) All the rest? Just smoke.

But the ghost has been joined by a few friends who take their places around the bed. Erdemovic shakes off Vesna and escapes.
The lights come up on the smoky bar. Erdemovic enters. He looks around. There are no ghosts present.

JULIJA: Well, Drazen. It's nice to see your face again.
ERDEMOVIC: Julija.

JULIJA: Such a pretty face. But not too pretty. I knew those acne scars would give you character.

She brings him a beer.

ERDEMOVIC: I know I can always rely on you, Julija, when my ego needs a boost. You certainly have a way with a compliment.

She laughs. He drinks most of the beer.

ERDEMOVIC: Have you seen Stanko around?
JULIJA: Not for weeks and weeks. I hear he's looking for work in Tuzla.
ERDEMOVIC: Good. I mean, well – good.
JULIJA: Something on your mind, Drazen?

He looks around again. Still no ghosts. He finishes the beer.

ERDEMOVIC: Julija, have you heard the stories about Srebrenica?
JULIJA: Who hasn't?
ERDEMOVIC: Do you believe them?
JULIJA: What? That eight to ten thousand Bosnian Muslim men are still missing?
ERDEMOVIC: And presumed dead. Do you believe such stories?
JULIJA: Of course I believe them. The Serbs commit horrible crimes against the Muslims. The Muslims commit horrible crimes against the Serbs. The Croats commit horrible crimes against both. What do you expect, Drazen? This is war. People do awful things. And life goes on.
ERDEMOVIC: Vesna doesn't believe it. Won't believe it.
JULIJA: Well.
ERDEMOVIC: I believe it. (softly) I was there.
JULIJA: So. (pause) Now what do you do?

ERDEMOVIC: What was it you said? "Life goes on." I try to get on with my life.
JULIJA: And that's why you're in here in a bar in the middle of the day.
ERDEMOVIC: I am trying, Julija. Trying as hard as I can. My father tells me that it's my duty to leave the war behind me now that I'm home. But it haunts my dreams. Every night. Vesna thinks I'm just imagining the horrors.
JULIJA: She's young. She's scared. She has a lot to lose. It's safer for her to believe your stories are nightmares.
ERDEMOVIC: They're not. They're real. They follow me day and night. I think I may be losing my mind.
JULIJA: Then do something about it. Cast out your demons.
ERDEMOVIC: You sound like a priest. Confess my sins to Father Zanic and my immortal soul will be washed clean of sin.
JULIJA: It works for some people.
ERDEMOVIC: But not for me.
JULIJA: You don't have to confess to a priest.
ERDEMOVIC: What do you mean?
JULIJA: Listen, Drazen. A French reporter has been sniffing around the village the past week. Have you seen him?
ERDEMOVIC: I haven't left the house for days.
JULIJA: Talk to him.
ERDEMOVIC: I don't think so.
JULIJA: Why not? Afraid of the wrath of Stanko?
ERDEMOVIC: Wouldn't you be?
JULIJA: What's the worst he can do to you? Kill you?
ERDEMOVIC: I have a wife and a family, Julija. I don't want to die.
JULIJA: A wife who thinks you're a madman and a child who thinks you're a monster. What kind of life is that, Drazen?
ERDEMOVIC: It's my life, Julija. The only one I have.
JULIJA: Fine. Then live your life, Drazen. Go home. Kiss your wife and son. Go!
ERDEMOVIC: You think my silence makes me a coward.
JULIJA: I didn't say that.

ERDEMOVIC: I *am* a coward. So what? Show me one human who's not a coward in his heart. Everyone thinks they will do the right thing when the time comes. They think "Oh, yes. I will be the one to rescue the woman being beaten by her husband. I'll be the one to catch the thief stealing from the fruit stand." But what do we really do? Stand there and hope like hell someone else will do it. Well, Julija, nobody else did a damned thing out there in that cornfield. And when it came right down to it, neither did I. Is it my fault I tried to save my life? Am I to be blamed for that? All I could think was, "I want to live. Dear God, let me live." It's not that I didn't think about them. Their faces staring at me, as if they expected me to do something. Stupid, stupid souls who believed the stories they were told. Believed they were going off to a prisoner of war camp. Marching off like sheep. Stupid. Stupid. There was one kid, younger than me. And he's looking at me when he figures out he's not going to any camp. That he's going to be dead in about 60 seconds. He just keeps looking at me. And I shoot him. Stanko was right. He said I was soft here, in my belly. He's right, Julija. I have no stomach for courage.
JULIJA: Then find some.
ERDEMOVIC: Not a problem. I'll pick some up at the corner chicken kiosk. They hang bags of courage right next to the dead roosters. Just to remind you the price of courage.
JULIJA: Is the price of fear such a bargain?
ERDEMOVIC: No. It's not. It eats away at me. Little by little. I hate myself for being afraid. I hate it. I truly hate it. (pause) Julija, suppose – suppose I wanted to talk to that French reporter? How could I find him?
JULIJA: I'll find him. What about tonight?
ERDEMOVIC: (losing his nerve) Tonight? No –
JULIJA: Tomorrow night, then. Late. You come back to the bar. See that table over there? That's where the "Le Figaro" reporter will be sitting. Will you be there? He'll wait for you.

There are the echoes of Erdemovic' ghosts.

GHOSTS: Erdemovic. Erdemovic! Erdemovic! Erdemovic!
ERDEMOVIC: (pause) He could be waiting a long time.

The ghosts continue their chant. And then there is silence.
We hear the sound of the three gavel strikes. The lights come up on the courtroom again.

JUDGE: Mr. Babic. You had one last question.

Babic walks over to the Plexiglas lectern.

BABIC: Yes, your honor. You have a wound, Mr. Erdemovic.
ERDEMOVIC: Yes, sir. Pieces of a shattered bullet are still in my stomach.
BABIC: Who shot you, Mr. Erdemovic?
ERDEMOVIC: One of my mates in the tenth sabotage unit.
BABIC: And what was the reason for the shooting, Mr. Erdemovic?
ERDEMOVIC: (he pauses) Someone had conveyed to the commander of my unit how I had behaved at the farm. And he probably reached the conclusion that I just couldn't stand it. And perhaps – I don't know – do what I'm doing today. Testifying.

Lights out on the courtroom. Lights up on the bar where Stanko, Brano & Aleksandar are gathered around a table, drinking and talking.

STANKO: So then I said to her, "I'll show you where we keep our spare ammunition. Right here *inside* our pants!"

They all laugh.

STANKO: Julija! Three slivos. Come meet my esteemed colleagues of the tenth sabotage!

She walks over to the table.

JULIJA: Stanko. So. You're back from Tuzla.
STANKO: No. I'm just a ghost come back to haunt you. Of course I'm back. Shake hands with the best commanding officer in Bosnia. Brano Gojkovic.
JULIJA: Commander.
BRANO: A pleasure, I'm sure.
JULIJA: And who's your other pal, Stanko?

He stands, clicks his heels, and bows.

ALEKSANDAR: Aleksandar Cvetkovic, at your service.
JULIJA: They take them young into the army, don't they?
ALEKSANDAR: I am fifteen years old. Old enough to kill. Old enough to drink.
JULIJA: Well, do your drinking and get yourselves out of here, fellows. The bar is closing early tonight.
STANKO: That's not like you, Julija. Here are three thirsty men with pockets full of deutschmarks, willing to spend every last one of them here tonight.
JULIJA: One more round and I'm closing up shop, Stanko.

She walks away.

BRANO: It is a nice town you have here, Stanko. Small, but nice.
ALEKSANDAR: I thought we were going to the discotheque.
BRANO: All in good time, my friend.

Julija returns with the tray of drinks and slams them on the table.

JULIJA: Drink up and go.
ALEKSANDAR: Hey. We don't have to take this. We can go to the discotheque.

STANKO: Shut up, Svetkovic. You act as if you have a lover waiting for you, Julija. Is that him? The fellow over there in the corner with the pencils?
JULIJA: I don't know what you're talking about.

Stanko pushes his chair away and walks over to another table, where a fellow sits quietly drinking a glass of beer.

STANKO: You. Pencil man. You have some business with Julija, here? A little rendezvous later on?
JULIJA: Leave my customers alone, Stanko.
REPORTER: I'll be back later, Mademoiselle. You know how to contact me.

He leaves the bar.

JULIJA: There. Are you satisfied?
STANKO: Not yet.
BRANO: Where is he, Mademoiselle?
JULIJA: Where is who?
BRANO: Don't play the fool. We know your boy Drazen was meeting that reporter tonight.
JULIJA: I don't know what you're talking about. Now, if you don't mind, I'm closing down for the night.

Julija starts to walk away. Stanko grabs her by the wrist.

STANKO: Always with the smart mouth, Julija.
JULIJA: Let me go.
STANKO: Too good for the rest of us.
JULIJA: You're hurting my arm.
STANKO: That's the general idea.

Julija reaches around with her other arm and slaps his face. Stanko and Aleksandar rise, knocking over a chair or two. Stanko slaps her back.

BRANO: Enough, Stanko.
ERDEMOVIC: (offstage) Julija. Sorry I'm late. Nevin is running a fever and I was trying to get him to swallow the apple syrup but-
BRANO: Get her out of here.

Stanko pushes her away. Erdemovic enters the bar, and freezes in his tracks when he sees the three men.

STANKO: Comrade. Welcome.
JULIJA: Run, Drazen. Run!
STANKO:(to Julija) Get out.

He pushes her out the door and stares at Erdemovic.

BRANO: Well. Good evening, Sgt. – no, sorry. I forgot you lost your rank for not following orders. Good evening, Private Erdemovic.
ERDEMOVIC: Commander Brano. Svetkovic. Stanko.
STANKO: It's practically a reunion of the entire tenth sabotage unit.
ERDEMOVIC: What do you want?
BRANO: Come drink with us, Drazen, my boy.

Stanko escorts Erdemovic to the table, stopping at the bar for a bottle and glasses. Brano indicates that Aleksandar should pour another drink. He does. The glass is passed to Erdemovic. Brano salutes him with his glass. And drinks.

Erdemovic does not drink.

BRANO: Well, well, well. Our little Drazen. Home at last. Comrade Stanko tells me your little boy is nearly a year old now. Sorry to hear he's not feeling well.
ERDEMOVIC: Yes. He has his father's stomach. What do you want, Commander?
BRANO: To talk over old times. Stanko tells me you're having bad dreams about certain activities of the tenth.
ERDEMOVIC: I'm all right.
BRANO: Glad to hear it. I, myself, have sleepless nights from time to time.
ALEKSANDAR: All those Turk women throwing themselves at you, eh, commander?
BRANO: Shut your mouth, Svetkovic. War is not a very pleasant thing, is it Drazen?
ERDEMOVIC: It's the worst kind of hell.
BRANO: And yet, you are not fighting for yourself, Drazen. You are fighting for a greater Serbia.
ERDEMOVIC: I don't care about politics.
BRANO: Ah, but you should.
ERDEMOVIC: I'm a Croat, not a Serb.
BRANO: Yes, and isn't that what was so wonderful about our small band of freedom fighters? Croat and Serb together, fighting against the infidels.
ERDEMOVIC: You talk like my father, discussing wars in the middle ages as if they were yesterday.
BRANO: Of course I am, you young fool. If you call yourself Yugoslav, you must live your history. Every day. How can you forget St. Vitus Day? The Battle of Kozovo. 1389 may sound like a hundred million years ago, but it's just yesterday for a Yugoslav. This is a country with a memory. A true Christian nation. God's country. Until the Turks marched in and slaughtered everyone in their wake. And that's just what the Muslims of Srebrenica were going to do to us if we had let them live.

ERDEMOVIC: You sound like all the propaganda that's spewed out over the radio. Propaganda from that mafia that led us into war. This was their war, not mine.
BRANO: Dangerous talk, comrade.
ERDEMOVIC: Those prisoners at Srebrenica. They were told they were going to prison camps. Would it be so bad to put them in prison instead of killing them all?
BRANO: Think, boy. Let them live and they'll breed more babies who will grow up to kill your young son. Listen to me, Drazen. You may think your actions had no meaning, but you're wrong. By shooting your gun in that cornfield, you saved the lives of thousands of others. Can you understand this? You were a hero.
ERDEMOVIC: Then why don't I feel like a hero?
BRANO: You're just tired, my boyo. Tired from all the fighting. It's good you came home to your family. It's good to forget all the fighting and the killing.
ERDEMOVIC: And if I can't forget?

There is a pause.

BRANO: That presents a bit of a dilemma…
STANKO: You were going to talk to that reporter, weren't you?
ALEKSANDAR: What reporter? Is that Julija's boyfriend with the pencils?
BRANO: You will close your mouth, Svetkovic, and you will not open it until I give you permission to do so. Drazen, I'm afraid we have a small problem here.
ERDEMOVIC: We have no problem here.
BRANO: When you joined the tenth sabotage unit, you knew the rules. Any soldier who threatens the security of the group can be executed on the spot. Drazen, I'm afraid you have become a danger to the group.
STANKO: If you talk, you could put all of us in danger.
ERDEMOVIC: Then I won't talk.
BRANO: I'm afraid we can't risk that, Drazen. Stanko?

Stanko pulls a gun from his holster. He cocks it.
Erdemovic rises and backs away.

ERDEMOVIC: Stanko, no!

He shoots three times.

ERDEMOVIC: Aahh!!
ALEKSANDAR: Jeez, he's bleeding all over me!
BRANO: I'm afraid this must be goodbye, Private. Come.
STANKO: Sorry, comrade. Maybe that will put a little iron in your gut.
ERDEMOVIC: Stanko. I'm bleeding. Help me.
STANKO: They were just stinking Turks, comrade. Nothing to get yourself upset about. Not worth dying over.

The men walk out, laughing. Erdemovic reaches out for help. A ghost enters and extends a hand. Erdemovic recoils in terror. The ghost slowly backs away. The lights change. Vesna enters and puts a pillow underneath Erdemovic' head. She covers him with a quilt and fusses with his bed. He grabs her hand, looks at it, and kisses it. Vesna is clearly uncomfortable and pulls her hand away.

VESNA: You'd better lie still or you'll reopen that wound again.
ERDEMOVIC: I'm all right. (pause) How are you? Vesna?

She doesn't answer.

ERDEMOVIC: Where's my little plumkin? Where is Nevin?
VESNA: He's at my mother's house for a few days. I don't want his crying to disturb you.

ERDEMOVIC: He won't disturb me.
VESNA: If he jumps on your bed, you'll start bleeding again and you will have to go back to the hospital.
ERDEMOVIC: That's not it. It's not my bleeding you're worried about. You don't want our child to come near me.
VESNA: You're talking crazy again.
ERDEMOVIC: It's true. Isn't it, Vesna? You're afraid of me now. You can see the blood on my hands. The blood in my gut.
VESNA: Drazen. You must try to put the war behind you. Let it go. You must try to live in the present.
ERDEMOVIC: Vesna. I must tell them.
VESNA: Tell who? Not that Tribunal business again.
ERDEMOVIC: All those weeks I was in the hospital, it's all anyone would talk about. A court for the massacres.
VESNA: And justice for all. You sound like one of those American courtroom dramas. What does this war crimes tribunal have to do with you?
ERDEMOVIC: I must tell them.
VESNA: Why? Why must you be the one to talk to them? Do you think Stanko and company will throw you a party to celebrate you telling your stories to this tribunal?
ERDEMOVIC: Someone has to know. Somebody has to tell the world.
VESNA: Why you? Think what could happen. Do you think this tribunal will say "thank you" after you tell them your story about killing people? Haven't you caused enough trouble for your family by trying to talk to that reporter?
ERDEMOVIC: Someone has to know the truth.
VESNA: Truth. Is that what you call it? Dreams. Nightmares.
ERDEMOVIC: Vesna.
VESNA: And even if it were true, what difference would it make? Will it bring one of those people back? No. All your truth-telling does is make people angry. Why couldn't you listened to me, Drazen? You should have forgotten those dreams.

ERDEMOVIC: You want me to forget those faces? Forget what I did? When you yourself can't forget. I see you, Vesna, watching me when you think I'm asleep.
VESNA: I don't know what you're talking about.
ERDEMOVIC: You ask yourself, "Who is this man?"
VESNA: You're imagining things.
ERDEMOVIC: Come. Prove it to me. Lay down beside me. Let me love you, Vesna.
VESNA: You're too weak, Drazen. Your wound will begin bleeding again.
ERDEMOVIC: It's the blood you're afraid of. That's true. But not mine. You're afraid of all those bleeding corpses. See? They're all around you.
VESNA: Stop it, Drazen! Stop it! Can't you see what you've done? You've ruined everything! Your stories have made you an untouchable. The village leper. No one will ever speak to us again. No one will invite us into their homes. Or share a meal with us. Or even buy us a drink. Do you know what someone called me yesterday? "Ustashe whore." Me! You did this, Drazen. You. Everybody knows the war was difficult and violent and bloody. But that was out there. On the battlefield. You brought your demons home, Drazen. You shoved them down people's throats. Even though you are the only one in the whole world telling such stories. People don't want to believe these things. We are civilized, modern people. Not monsters. You're the monster, Drazen. You.
ERDEMOVIC: Yes, it's true. I count only corpses as my friends. You see? They don't scare me anymore. So long as I speak the truth, they can't harm me.
VESNA: You're mad, Drazen. Crazy.
ERDEMOVIC: Don't you see, Vesna? I must speak the truth. Or lose my very soul. I must speak the truth.
VESNA: No!

She leaves the stage and returns with a suitcase. She leaves and returns with a coat.

ERDEMOVIC: What are you doing?
VESNA: I am going home to stay with my parents.
ERDEMOVIC: Vesna. Don't leave me. Please.
VESNA: Everything has changed, Drazen. Everything.
ERDEMOVIC: My son?
VESNA: He is staying with me.
ERDEMOVIC: Vesna, please. I will stop talking about the war. Stop talking this crazy talk.
VESNA: I will send someone over to check on you every day to make sure you have not bled to death. And to leave you a bit of soup or something to eat.
ERDEMOVIC: Vesna, wait. You were right. I made it all up. It never happened. I was just trying to get even with Stanko.
VESNA: Goodbye, Drazen.
ERDEMOVIC: My unit was just a patrol unit. We never even saw any action. Vesna!

She exits. We hear the door slam.

ERDEMOVIC: Vesna. Vesna. Vesna.

The lights change again. Erdemovic is back in his prison cell. The guard returns.

GUARD: Lunch time.
ERDEMOVIC: Not hungry.
GUARD: I wrote another letter to your wife.
ERDEMOVIC: Let me guess. It came back in little pieces.
GUARD: I'm sure she'll answer this one.
ERDEMOVIC: I'm sure she won't. Enough talk about Vesna. I'm sick of talking. It's your turn.
GUARD: My turn? All right.
ERDEMOVIC: So, Officer Elsbeth Van der Kellen, what's a nice Dutch girl like you doing in this medieval prison?

GUARD: (she shrugs her shoulders) I finished up my army service and needed a job. A few of my pals heard the U.N. was paying good money for security personnel. Even built a private gym for the guards in the basement of the Tribunal building. Sounded interesting, babysitting accused war criminals. So I signed up. End of story.
ERDEMOVIC: Babysitting. Thanks. Where did you serve in the army?
GUARD: No place interesting. But my brother served in Bosnia.
ERDEMOVIC: Really? Where?

There is a pause.

GUARD: Srebrenica.
ERDEMOVIC: Quite a coincidence.
GUARD: Not really. I requested this duty. I could have stood around in the courtroom all day. But here, at least, they let you talk to the prisoners.
ERDEMOVIC: And you wanted to talk to me?

She nods.

ERDEMOVIC: Why?
GUARD: I wanted to know what I would have done if I were in your shoes.
ERDEMOVIC: You would shoot.

She stiffens and is silent.

ERDEMOVIC: I'm sorry. Talk to me, Elsbeth Van der Kellen. (she does not respond) Your brother – what's his name?
GUARD: Willem. He was a year older than me. Whatever Willem did, I wanted to do the same. He rode his bicycle to Maastricht, I rode my bicycle to Maastricht. He joined the army, I joined the army. He went to Srebrenica to meet Yugoslavs, I'm here in Scheveningen talking to you. (pause)

GUARD: (cont) Willem was with the Dutch Peacekeeping forces guarding the U.N. safe area.
ERDEMOVIC: He must have felt very proud of himself. Helping to separate men from women, helping to load the busses that brought the men to the killing field.
GUARD: It wasn't his fault! The Serbs had surrounded Srebrenica. Willem's garrison had shrunk to 400 men. Four hundred to protect 25 thousand! It couldn't be done!
ERDEMOVIC: Then the U.N. had no business promising something it had no intention of carrying out.
GUARD: My brother wasn't the one who pulled the trigger that killed those people.
ERDEMOVIC: No. Those were my orders.
GUARD: (pause) When Willem came home, he and the rest of the Dutch peacekeepers were considered heroes. Some of his mates were taken as human shields, you know. Not Willem. But he was a hero in my father's eyes anyway. They all were. Until the truth leaked out. Suddenly the Dutch heroes were labeled collaborators and cowards and criminals.
ERDEMOVIC: And what did Willem say about what happened?
GUARD: He never said anything. He never talked about Srebrenica. After a while, he stopped talking at all. He hung around with his mates, mostly. Drinking. He was drunk that night. It was in January. It wasn't cold enough to freeze the canals, but the roads were icy. Willem slipped on the ice and fell off his bicycle. They found his body in the Mauritskade canal. They say he killed himself. I don't believe it.
ERDEMOVIC: I'm sorry.
ELSBETH: So am I. Why are you the only one in court, Drazen Erdemovic? Why isn't your commanding officer on trial? Where are the other men who pulled the trigger?
STANKO: Yeah. Where are your old comrades?

Stanko enters and sits beside him in the prison cell.

ERDEMOVIC: Stanko!
STANKO: It's me, old friend.
GUARD: Who are you talking to?
ERDEMOVIC: Stanko! I knew you'd find me here.
GUARD: There's nobody here but me, kiddo.
ERDEMOVIC: Why have you come back? To finish the job?
STANKO: Too easy. Shooting you is like shooting fish in a barrel.
GUARD: Hey, Erdemovic. Snap out of it!

She pounds on the bars. Erdemovic notices her and tries to ignore Stanko.

GUARD: You okay, kiddo?
ERDEMOVIC: Yeah. Fine. Thanks. Just another afternoon nightmare. I'm okay now.
STANKO: Sure you are.
ERDEMOVIC: (to Stanko) Just go away.
GUARD: Okay, okay. If that's what you want. See you later, kiddo.

She exits.

STANKO: Pretty girl, comrade. But then, you've always had the pretty girls, haven't you? Vesna. Julija. Elsbeth.
ERDEMOVIC: Why don't you leave me alone?
STANKO: Hey, it's either me or the guys with bullet holes.
ERDEMOVIC: What do you mean?
STANKO: You wanna share your cell with a bunch of stinkin' Turks?

He laughs and laughs. Again, the lights change. Erdemovic pulls a bottle and a glass from his pillow. He staggers over to the kitchen table and sits. And drinks. His ghosts – more of them this time – appear as well and sit around the stage. A rooster crows three times.

ERDEMOVIC: Oh, shut up.

He pours another glass. And staggers over to a telephone. He dials. He is drunk.

TELEPHONE OPERATOR: (on phone) Dobro jutro. Good morning, American Embassy.
ERDEMOVIC: Hello American Embassy. I want to speak please to -
TELEPHONE OPERATOR: One moment please.

We hear bad music on hold. Erdemovic keeps on talking.

ERDEMOVIC: Hello. Hello! I want to speak to your United Nations Tribunal.
TELEPHONE OPERATOR: Good morning, American Embassy. How may I help you?
ERDEMOVIC: I have important evidence for this Yugoslav Tribunal.
TELEPHONE OPERATOR: I'm sorry, sir. The International Criminal Tribunal for the Former Yugoslavia is located in The Hague.
ERDEMOVIC: In the where?
TELEPHONE OPERATOR: In The Hague. In The Netherlands.
ERDEMOVIC: Well, give me the number for the Belgrade office.
TELEPHONE OPERATOR: Sir, there is no Belgrade office.
ERDEMOVIC: Listen to me. I have a story you must hear. Will you listen to me?

Julija enters.

TELEPHONE OPERATOR: Uh, sir, I have other calls to take.
ERDEMOVIC: You must listen to my story. Please!
JULIJA: Drazen.

ERDEMOVIC: Julija. They won't listen to my story. No one will listen to my story.

She takes the phone from his hands. He cries. Wipes his nose. Pours himself another drink.

JULIJA: Haven't you ever heard that drinking alone is one of the signs of an alcoholic?
EDEMOVIC: (toasting) To the alcoholic!
JULIJA: I heard you were holed up here all by yourself.
ERDEMOVIC: Vesna is – just visiting her family for a few days.
JULIJA: That's what I hear. Are you all right?
ERDEMOVIC: I'm surviving. It will take more than a few bullet fragments to kill me. Just means I can't drink the way I used to.
JULIJA: You never drank the way you used to. You got another glass? Never mind.

She drinks from the bottle.

ERDEMOVIC: It's good to see you again, Julija. You don't think I'm an ogre, do you?
JULIJA: An ogre? You? You were always a scared little boy, Drazen. A crybaby. But not an ogre.
ERDEMOVIC: I can live with crybaby. To the crybaby!
JULIJA: To the crybaby.

They clink his glass to her bottle. There is an awkward pause.

JULIJA: So.
ERDEMOVIC: I miss my son.
JULIJA: But not your wife.
ERDEMOVIC: "The most beautiful girl in the obstina." (after a moment) <u>You</u> are beautiful, Julija.
JULIJA: And you are very drunk.

ERDEMOVIC: Yes, I am. But you are still very beautiful, Julija.

She considers him for a moment. And kisses him full on the lips.

JULIJA: Here.

She slaps a piece of paper into his hand and turns to leave.

ERDEMOVIC: What is it?
JULIJA: Call that number before you sober up.

She exits. He reads the paper and dials. A phone rings. Lights up on a young reporter.

PHILIP: ABC News.
ERDEMOVIC: Hello?
PHILIP: Yes?

There is a click on the line.

PHILIP: (to himself) Damn phones. So much clicking and clucking on the line you'd think chickens were running the telephone company. (back to phone) Yes? Hello?
ERDEMOVIC: Yes, I have a story you might be interested in hearing.
PHILIP: Yes? Who is this please?
ERDEMOVIC: You have heard of Srebrenica? I was there.
PHILIP: (pause) Where can I meet you?

The stage grows dark. We hear crickets and perhaps an owl. Erdemovic is nearly sober by now. But here and there, a ghost lurks in the dark shadows. Sitting on a log is a young journalist, Philip.

With him is a bored cameraman who will film the interview. We see the close-up of Erdemovic on the TV screen.

PHILIP: So, Mr. Erdemovic. How many men were there in this special squad, the – what did you call it?
ERDEMOVIC: The Tenth Sabotage Detachment of the Bosnian Serb Army. There were 80 of us. Serbs. Croats. Even a few Muslims.
PHILIP: Did you have some sort of official mission?
ERDEMOVIC: It was after the fall of Srebrenica.
PHILIP: You were one of the soldiers attacking the so-called U.N. safe area?
ERDEMOVIC: I was one of the soldiers who finished what they started. (pause) Did you ever wonder how much blood a patch of earth can absorb before it turns into a small lake?
PHILIP: Can't say that I have.
ERDEMOVIC: I can tell you. About three bodies worth of blood. Then the earth can absorb no more. My unit was assigned to a farm near Pilica.
PHILIP: Go on.
ERDEMOVIC: It was a hot day. No wind. The cornstalks were taller than a man. They showed us how to shoot our guns without wasting bullets so we could execute as many people as possible in a very short period of time.
PHILIP: How many people?
ERDEMOVIC: I don't know how many. Busloads and busloads. Maybe twelve hundred men. Some of them were very young. 17 to 18 years old. The soldiers from the other unit cursed them. Called them Turks and worse. Beat them with metal bars. They didn't say a word. But when the second bus arrived, the men saw the bodies. Some cried out to us.

Stanko and Aleksandar appear at one side of the stage. The ghosts line up.

GHOST: Allahu akbar. God is great! Please! Don't kill us! Our families in Austria will bring us money!
STANKO: Whoever has two marks will save himself. Get out the money.
GHOST: We have already emptied our pockets.
STANKO: Resume firing.
ERDEMOVIC: I tried not to shoot at the youngest. I don't think that I killed more than a total of 70 prisoners. Maybe less. At one point, I told one of my comrades, "God knows everything we've done today."
STANKO: Shut up and shoot!
ERDEMOVIC: Even the bus drivers were forced to kill someone. They had no idea they were driving their busses to the execution grounds. They thought they were part of a prisoner exchange. The commander gave his rifle to a driver.

Brano enters, pushing along a Bus Driver. He hands him his gun.

BRANO: Shoot one of them.
BUS DRIVER: No. No!
BRANO: Go on. Pick one. Pick two. Kill them. Do it.

Lights go out on Brano and the Bus Driver and on Erdemovic and the reporter. There is the sound of shots and grenades exploding. And screams. They fade out. We hear a cough or two.
A blank white slide is shown on the back wall. No picture. The prosecutor steps in front of the light, so all we see is him in profile.

PROSECUTOR: Later that same day, the 10th Sabotage Unit was ordered to the town of Pilica where an additional 500 Muslim men were being held inside town meeting hall.

PROSECUTOR: (cont) Now, exhibit number nine – in this photograph, we can see the inside of the building in which the executions are alleged to have taken place. The definition of the image is not very good, but inside the building, there were traces of bullet impacts, which can be seen on all the walls, on the floor and on the platform.

We hear the sound of a slide changing. The lights flicker, but again, it is a blank, white slide. No picture.

PROSECUTOR: Exhibit number eleven shows the traces of blood with bits of hair as well. The ceiling was also splattered with all kinds of substances – probably from human beings, but for which the analysis has not yet been completed.

The slides change again. Again, no picture.

PROSECUTOR: Exhibit 13 is a view of the back of the room, behind the podium. Certain parts of that podium have been destroyed because it appears that there were grenade explosions there.

The "slide" light goes out. The Prosecutor addresses the court.

PROSECUTOR: All of the statements made by Drazen Erdemovic have been confirmed by the observations we were able to carry out on site. Your honors, before Drazen Erdemovic, the prosecution had no knowledge of these events.

We hear a knock on a door. Lights out on the Prosecutor. When the lights come up, Erdemovic is down center in the space used for his jail cell. Father appears in the place up center where the Judge usually sits.

ERDEMOVIC: Father. Father?
FATHER: So. The media star shows his face.
ERDEMOVIC: May I come inside?
FATHER: What for?
ERDEMOVIC: Is mother home?
FATHER: Sylvana saw your mother at the chicken kiosk. You know Sylvana and her fancy satellite dish and her American soap operas. Imagine her surprise when the famous CNN news anchor starts talking about Drazen Erdemovic! So naturally Sylvana rushes to tell your mother. Such a thing for your mother to hear from the neighbors! Her son, the murderer!
ERDEMOVIC: Father. I did not want to do these things.
FATHER: But you did them anyway.
ERDEMOVIC: I had no choice!
FATHER: Your arguments are those of a child. Grow up, Drazen. You made your own choices. You chose to leave the Croatian army. You chose to smuggle Serbs across the border. You could have chosen not to shoot your gun.
ERDEMOVIC: I tried!
FATHER: You tried.
ERDEMOVIC: At first I resisted. I told him I am no robot for the extermination of people. But my commander said if I was so sorry for those people I should line up with them and be shot.
FATHER: Better a dead son than a living piece of shit. Go away, Drazen. Go away.
ERDEMOVIC: Father!
FATHER: Go away.

Lights go out on Father. A telephone rings. Lights up on stage left where Philip stands with a phone in his hand.

ERDEMOVIC: Hello?

PHILIP: (on the phone) Drazen, it's me. Philip.
Listen to me! You've got to get out. Now. My tapes were confiscated at the airport. My telephone must have been tapped. Get out. Now!

We hear soldiers pounding at the door.

SOLDIER:(off stage) Drazen Erdemovic?
ERDEMOVIC: What do you want?
SOLDIER:(off stage) Drazen Erdemovic. You are under arrest by order of the Federal Republic of Yugoslavia. Open the door!

The lights fade as the pounding continues. Over the pounding, we hear the familiar three taps of the Tribunal courtroom gavel. Lights come up on the Judge, who is back in her customary place.

JUDGE: Mr. Erdemovic. Tell us please. Why did you decide to testify before this Tribunal? What feelings underlie your decision?

The lights go out on the judge, once again leaving Erdemovic alone on stage.

ERDEMOVIC: I wanted to testify because of my conscience. Because of all that happened. Because I did not want that. I was simply compelled to, forced to. And I could choose between my life and the lives of those people. And had I lost my life then, it would not have changed the fate of those people. The fate of those people was decided by someone holding a much higher position than I did. And as I have said already – what really got me – it's completely destroyed my life. That is why I testified.

Lights change. Erdemovic is once again in his jail cell. The Guard enters with Vesna.

ERDEMOVIC: Vesna? Is it really you?

Erdemovic reaches out, trying to touch her through the bars.

GUARD: Hold on a minute, kiddo. Let me get the door open.

The Guard unlocks the door.

ERDEMOVIC: Vesna!

They embrace. Vesna is stiff.

VESNA: Hello, Drazen. You're so pale.
GUARD: Congratulations, kiddo. I told you she'd come. I'll be right outside.
ERDEMOVIC: Vesna. You came. You're here.
VESNA: We saw you on television, Drazen. Nevin and I. At Sylvana's house in the village. We saw you testify in court.
ERDEMOVIC: It's so good to see you, to touch you, Vesna.
VESNA: It's funny. On Serbian TV, they call you a traitor. On Muslim TV, they call you "the brave one who speaks."
ERDEMOVIC: What do you call me, Vesna? Do you call me husband?
VESNA: Your attorney, Mr. Babic, asked me to come to court. He thought it would help your case.
ERDEMOVIC: Vesna, I love you.
VESNA: You look so different on television, Drazen. Taller. Almost like a soap opera star.
ERDEMOVIC: Vesna, tell me everything that's happened since I've been gone. Have you talked to my parents?

She remembers the package in her hand.

VESNA: Your mother baked you a plum cake. (he takes it) Drazen, I told Mr. Babic I will testify for you in court if he needs me.

ERDEMOVIC: That's very good news.
VESNA: And in exchange, you will do something for me.
ERDEMOVIC: Anything, my Vesna. Anything.
VESNA: I want an annulment.
ERDEMOVIC: A what? An annulment? What?
VESNA: Fr. Zanic says in light of your confessed crimes, you cannot have been a sane man. And with your cooperation, an annulment will be relatively simple.
ERDEMOVIC: Vesna, no.
VESNA: I will live with my parents for a time. They will help with Nevin while I find a job and go on with my life.
ERDEMOVIC: Vesna, please wait. Mr. Babic says I have a good chance of being set free, of serving no more time in prison.
VESNA: And what if you have run out of good chances? Am I supposed to sit at home and grow old and ugly waiting for you? Work to provide for our son all by myself? Our life is ruined, Drazen. Ruined. And all because you could not leave well enough alone. All because you could not keep your mouth shut about Pilica.
ERDEMOVIC: Vesna.
VESNA: My parents were right. You are cursed, Drazen. And it is not my responsibility to wait for you. Goodbye. Guard! Guard, I am ready to leave.
ERDEMOVIC: Vesna, please. Vesna! Vesna!!

The Guard opens the door.

VESNA: It's time to go. Goodbye, Drazen. Good luck in court.

She walks away.

ERDEMOVIC: Vesna!

Once again, we hear three slow taps of a gavel on wood. The lawyers take their places in the courtroom. So do the ghosts.

The judge appears upstage.

BAILIFF: The International Criminal Tribunal for the Former Yugoslavia is now in session. Please be seated.

PROSECUTOR: Your honors. The defendant before you, Drazen Erdemovic, will be the first person to be sentenced before an international criminal tribunal in 50 years. Mr. Erdemovic has pleaded guilty to a crime against humanity. The underlying facts of which are undisputed. Exactly how many people Mr. Erdemovic personally killed, I cannot tell you. I do not know. Mr. Erdemovic may not know. Only God knows. In every national jurisdiction, the taking of a life or of lives by another is punished by the severest of sanctions. In this court, the maximum punishment that Mr. Erdemovic faces is life imprisonment term. Were Mr. Erdemovic the one who planned, organized or instigated this monstrous crime, my recommendation to you would be simple and direct: impose a life sentence. That will not be my recommendation to you. In this case, Mr. Erdemovic, a low-ranking member of the Bosnian Serb army, followed orders – albeit patently illegal orders – of a superior to execute innocent civilians. He says he did so out of fear for his life. You may consider these as mitigating circumstances and give them whatever weight you deem appropriate. Let me very clear on this point: Mr. Erdemovic has provided substantial assistance to the prosecutors' office in relation to the investigations of Srebrenica. His cooperation was and continues to be unconditional. I will tell your honors quite frankly: his assistance to us has been invaluable. Your honors, the prosecutor recommends leniency in the case of Mr. Erdemovic.

JUDGE: Thank you prosecution. I now give the floor to you, Mr. Babic.

BABIC: Your honors. When I first contemplated the defense of the accused Erdemovic, I silently scanned the titles of books in my library. My eyes lingered and my mind came awake at the title "The Naked and the Dead." This is a novel that you all know – a novel by the American author Norman Mailer, a book that paints a hardened picture of war.

BABIC: (cont) But this is also a book filled with yearning for the peaceful sleep without suffering, blood, mud, and insomnia. The title reminded me forcibly of the fate of man in the cruel war in the former Yugoslavia: the fate of my client, a man who is a victim of his own deed. At the Nuremberg Trials, 22 people were tried, the main war criminals of fascist Germany. 12 were sentenced to death. Three to life in prison. And 4 to imprisonment from 10 to 20 years. And three were acquitted. It is well known that this was the political and military leadership of Germany whose crimes had killed millions of people and brought awful terrors to the world. The accused Erdemovic is not a field marshal, nor any kind of military commander. He was a plain soldier. He had to obey orders and not his conscience. He could not resist the order in any possible way. I believe it is not moral to expect that he should have sacrificed his own life first, and then quite certainly, the life of his family, too. Therefore, your honors, I request that he be acquitted. Thank you.
JUDGE: Thank you, Mr. Babic. Mr. Erdemovic, is there anything you would like to add?
ERDEMOVIC: Yes. First of all, honorable judges, I wish to say that I feel sorry for all the victims. Not only for the ones who were killed then at that farm, I feel sorry for all the victims in the former Bosnia and Herzegovina, regardless of their nationality. Mr. Babic, when he first arrived here, he told me, "Drazen, can you change your decision? I don't know what can happen?" I told him because of those victims, because of my conscience, because of my life, because of my child and my wife, I cannot change what I said. Because of the peace of my mind, my soul, my honesty because of the victims of war, because of everything. Because of everything that happened, I feel terribly sorry. But I could not do anything. When I could do something, I did it. I have nothing else to say.
JUDGE: Very well. Mr. Erdemovic. Having considered all of the facts of the case submitted for its attention, the trial chamber sentences Drazen Erdemovic to ten years imprisonment. This judgment shall be enforceable immediately, today, 29 November, 1996, The Hague, The Netherlands. The hearing is closed.

BAILIFF: All rise.
ERDEMOVIC: Ten years. Ten years!
BABIC: Calm yourself. Please, Drazen. It is a surprise, yes. But we will appeal. The court refused to take into account the extreme necessity. The fact that you had no choice. That is certainly a strong basis for appeal.

We hear the voice of Stanko.

STANKO: (laughing) You should have kept your mouth shut, comrade.
BABIC: I'll come see you tomorrow and we'll talk about our next step. Hold onto your courage, Drazen. This is not the end of our struggle. Good bye, my boy.

He shakes hands with Erdemovic and joins the cast in their ghost masks.

ERDEMOVIC: It is finished. (he turns to the ghosts) And you. Are you satisfied? I told them your story. I told the world. Is it enough?

The ghosts bow in unison. One by one they turn their "face" away from Erdemovic. He is truly alone.

ERDEMOVIC: Free. I'm free.

The lights slowly fade to black.

A BRIEF HISTORY OF YUGOSLAVIA

Conventional wisdom holds that it was ancient religious rivalries that led to the outbreak of violence in Yugoslavia in the 1990's. Not so. It was said of Bosnia that even back in the 14th century, the country was an "example to Europe of how people of different religions could live together in harmony."

But there has been ethnic violence over the years. On June 28th, 1389, St. Vitus Day, Turkish Muslims fought Orthodox Christian Serbs at the Battle of Kosovo and then occupied much of Yugoslavia. It was a day that would live on in numerous anniversaries.

Five hundred years later, in 1876, Serb allegations of Muslim cruelty led to war with Turkey. Twelve thousand Orthodox Christians were killed in nearby Bulgaria. Russians (including the fictional Count Vronsky from Tolstoy's *Anna Karenina)* rushed to volunteer to fight in the Serb army. When the war was over two years later, Bosnia became part of the Austria-Hungarian empire.

On June 28, 1914, again on St. Vitus Day, a Bosnian Serb fired the shot that began the first World War. Serb casualties during the war were two and a half times greater than even those suffered by the

French. The treaty that ended the war was signed at Versailles – again, on St. Vitus Day.

It established the Kingdom of Serbs, Croats and Slovenes – or SHS. No one was happy. The Roman Catholic Croats called it "the Serbs want it all." The Serbs called it "only the Croats spoil it." In 1929, King Alexander banned all political parties. Five years later, he was assassinated by Croatian nationalists known as the Ustashe.

The second World War did much to truly divide Yugoslavia. It was said that Hitler hated the Serbs second only to the Jews. Croats sided with the Germans and were accused of committing atrocities that even the Nazis found appalling. Serbs were forced to wear blue armbands with the letter "P" on them. Orthodox priests were massacred. And on St. Vitus Day, at a Franciscan monastery near Medjugorje – the place where believers say the Virgin Mary appeared in the 1980's – six hundred women and children were thrown off a cliff.

After the war, Marshal Tito and communism came to power and there was no discussion of the war crimes of World War Two. Officially under communism, there was also no practice of religion. In many ways, this enforced "can't we all just get along" policy worked. In larger cities like Sarajevo, Serbs, Croats and Muslims intermarried. In smaller cities, neighbors worked together to build a new roof or act as pallbearers at a funeral. No one asked whether you were Serb, Croat, or Muslim.

But after the fall of communism, political leaders were looking for a way to strengthen their power. The state still controlled the media, a holdover from communist days. So leaders used the airwaves and television channels to broadcast a message of hate 24 hours a day, for several years – that "they" were out to take your job, that "they" were having too many children, that "they" were stockpiling weapons and planning to come kill you. What resulted was the slaughter of civilians, the rape of girls as young as 12 years of age, and the destruction of churches and libraries and villages.

The international community was slow to respond to the crisis in Bosnia. But after the fighting, the U.N. dusted off the international law books and created the International Criminal Tribunal for the Former Yugoslavia (ICTY) and its sister tribunal for Rwanda. It was the first time since the Nuremberg and Tokyo Trials after World War Two that individuals would be held responsible by the international community for war crimes. So far, 59 individuals have been publicly indicted. But because the Tribunal has no police force of its own and must rely on other countries or NATO troops to make arrests, more than half of these suspects are still at large.

The first man to be tried by the ICTY in 1996 was a karate teacher named Dusan Tadic. After a nine month trial, he was found guilty of acting as a freelance terrorist, entering prison camps at will, and savagely beating his former neighbors.

Drazen Erdemovic was the first man to be sentenced by the Tribunal. There was no trial: he simply pleaded guilty and was sentenced to ten years in prison. Lawyers for Drazen Erdemovic successfully appealed and his sentence was reduced to five years behind bars. He was released in 2000.

PROGRAM NOTES

The courtroom scenes in A PATCH OF EARTH are taken directly from transcripts of the International Criminal Tribunal for the Former Yugoslavia. The facts of his case are true. The personal and family life of Erdemovic in A PATCH OF EARTH have been created from the playwright's imagination.

ABOUT THE PLAY

A Patch of Earth has won the Maxim Mazumdar New Play Competition, was a finalist for the William P. & Arlene R. Lewis Playwriting Contest, and earned an Honorable Mention in the Writers' Digest Playwriting Contest. The play has been part of the curriculum at Portland Community College. It is included in the collection *The Theatre of Genocide: Four Plays About Mass Murder in Rwanda, Bosnia, Cambodia, and Armenia* (University of Wisconsin Press). The play has been produced worldwide and broadcast on Orange County's PBS station KOCE.

ABOUT THE PLAYWRIGHT

Kitty Felde covered the trial of Drazen Erdemovic at the International Criminal Tribunal for the former Yugoslavia for public radio. When she returned to the United States, his story kept haunting her, much as the ghosts in the play haunt Drazen. She wrote *A Patch of Earth* to satisfy those ghosts.

Kitty's other plays include *Gogol Project*, commissioned by the Rogue Artists Ensemble in Los Angeles, and winner of the LA Drama Critics Award for best adaptation. She often writes about the Theodore Roosevelt family. Her one-woman show *Alice* premiered at The National Theatre in Washington, D.C., played at NYC's Miranda Theatre, and was The Washington Post's "critic's pick" at the Capital Fringe Fest. A one-man show about the youngest son *Quentin* plays as a tour around the White House.

She also writes The Fina Mendoza Mysteries series of middle grade novels and podcasts, designed to introduce civics to kids.

Kitty is a veteran public radio reporter and talk show host, named "Journalist of the Year" three times in three years by the LA Press Club and Society of Professional Journalists. She covered Capitol Hill for nearly a decade. Kitty is currently host and executive producer of the award-winning *Book Club for Kids* podcast.

www.kittyfelde.com

Made in United States
North Haven, CT
04 November 2026

21772483R00046